BUG BOOKS

Mosquito

Jill Bailey

Heinemann Library
Chicago, Illinois

Customer Service 888-454-2279
Visit our website at www.heinemannraintree.com

Designed by Ron Kamen, Michelle Lisseter, and Bridge Creative Services Limited
Illustrations by Alan Fraser at Pennant Illustration
Printed in China

15 14 13
10 9 8 7

New edition ISBN: 1-4034-8300-0 (hardcover)
                  1-4034-8313-2 (paperback)

The Library of Congress has cataloged the first edition as follows:
Bailey, Jill.
    Mosquito/ Jill Bailey.
        p. cm. -- (Bug Books)
    Includes bibliographical references and index.
    Summary: A simple introduction to the physical characteristics, diet, life cycle, predators,
            habitat, and lifespan of mosquitoes.
    ISBN 1-57572-663-7 (lib. bdg.)
    ISBN 978-1-4034-8300-3 (HC)   ISBN 978-1-4034-8313-3 (Pbk.)
    1. Mosquitoes—Juvenile literature. [1. Mosquitoes.] I. Title. II. Series.
QL536.B2 1998
595.77'2—dc21   98-10596
                     CIP
                     AC

Acknowledgments
The author and publishers are grateful to the following for permission to reproduce photographs: Ardea London Ltd pp. 21 (R Gibbons), 4 (D Greenslade); Bruce Coleman Ltd pp. 20 (J Shaw), 23 (K Taylor); FLPA pp. 25 (D Gewcock), 15 (L West); Chris Honeywell p. 28; naturepl.com p. 18 (M Durham); NHPA pp. 9, 11, 14 (G Bernard), 17, 19, 24 (S Dalton), 7 (P Parks); Oxford Scientific Films pp. 16 (R Brown), 6, 8, 10, 12, 13 (J Cooke); London Scientific Films:pp. 22; 29 (H Taylor); Planet Earth Pictures p. 26 (A Mounter); Science Photo Library pp. 5 (T Brain), 27 (A Crump).

Cover photograph reproduced with permission of Getty Images/The Image Bank.

The publishers would like to thank Nancy Harris for her assistance in the preparation of this book.

Every effort has been made to contact copyright holders of any material reproduced in this book. Any omissions will be rectified in subsequent printings if notice is given to the publisher.

The paper used to print this book comes from sustainable sources.

Some words are shown in bold, **like this**. You can find out what they mean by looking in the glossary.

Contents

What Are Mosquitoes?

Mosquitoes are **insects**. They have a body made up of three parts. They have six legs and two wings.

A mosquito has big eyes. It has **feelers** on its head for touching, smelling, and hearing. Baby mosquitoes are small and wriggly. They live in water.

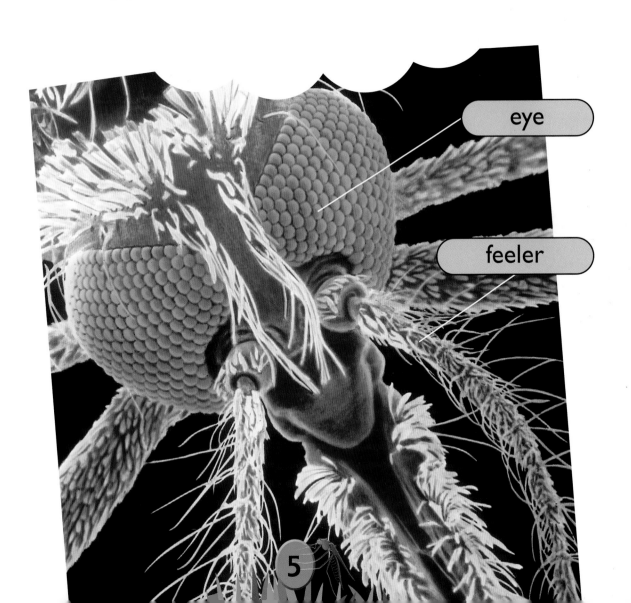

eye

feeler

What Do Mosquitoes Look Like?

Mosquitoes are very small. The common house mosquito is only as long as your little fingernail.

Mosquitoes fly in a jerky up-and-down way. Their legs hang below them as they fly. When they rest, they fold their wings.

How Are Mosquitoes Born?

The **female** house mosquito lays lots of eggs on the surface of a small pool or puddle. The eggs float on the water.

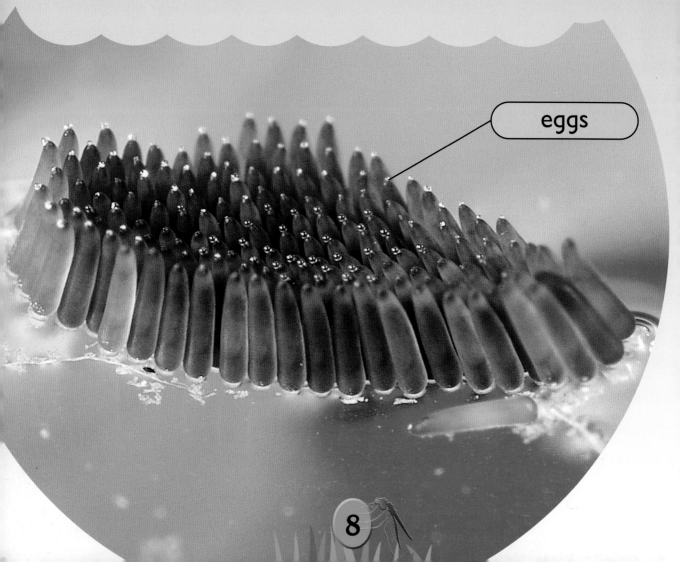

eggs

After a few hours, the eggs **hatch**.
Tiny, wriggling babies called **larvae**
wriggle out and swim away.

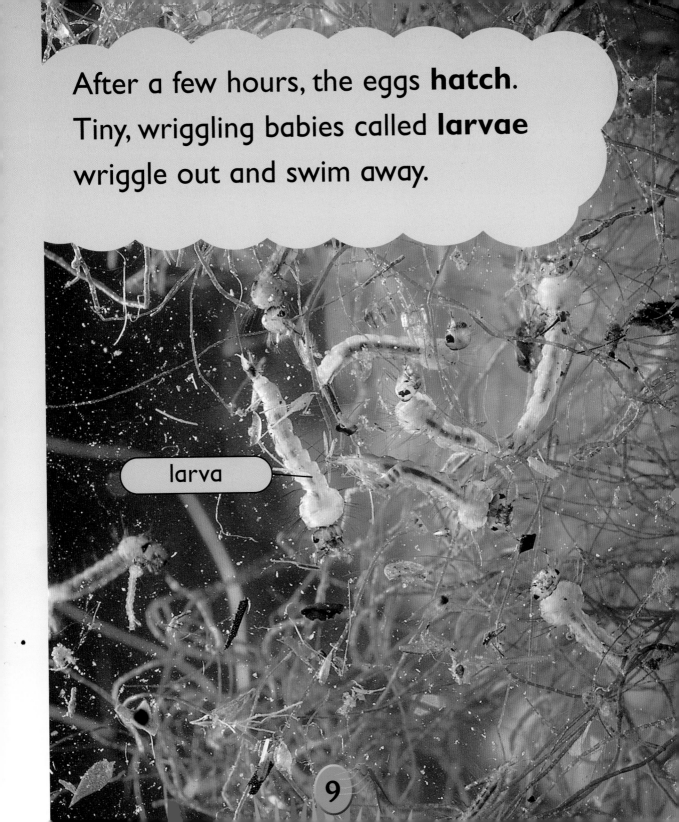

larva

How Do Mosquitoes Grow?

The mosquito **larvae** hang upside-down from the water's surface. They breathe in air through a long tube.

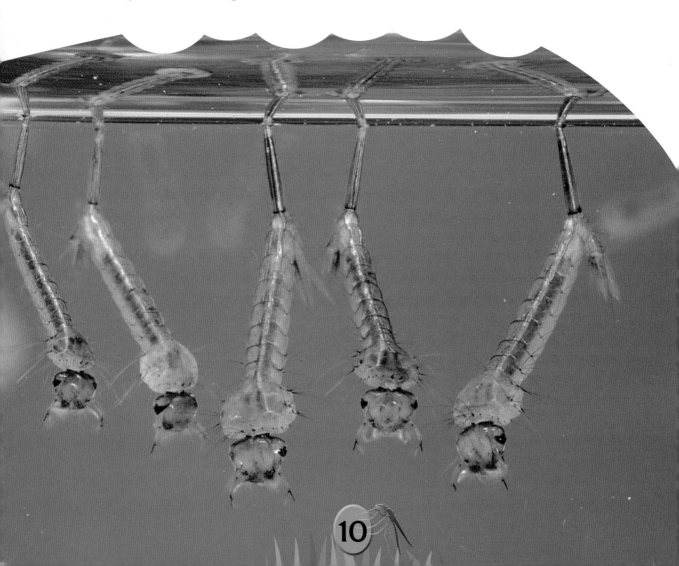

A larva's mouth is surrounded by hairs.
These hairs sweep water into its
mouth. The larva eats tiny pieces of
food that float in the water.

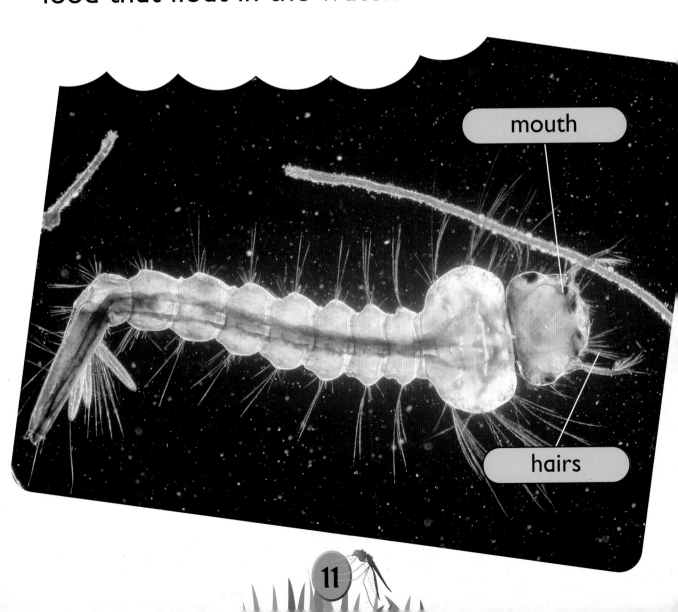

mouth

hairs

When a **larva** gets big enough it
stops eating. Its head end gets very
large. It is now called a **pupa**.

Inside its skin, the pupa slowly changes
into an adult mosquito. The skin splits.
The new mosquito climbs
out and flies away.

What Do Mosquitoes Eat?

Adult mosquitoes suck up flower **nectar** through their long mouths. **Female** mosquitoes drink blood from people or animals to help them make eggs.

The female mosquito breaks the skin of an animal or person with her sharp mouth. Then she adds a juice to keep the blood from **clotting** as she feeds. This juice can make the bite itch.

Which Animals Attack Mosquitoes?

Many birds eat mosquitoes. They sometimes feed them to their babies.

Frogs, toads, rats, and mice also eat mosquitoes. Spiders catch them in their webs. Fish, water beetles, and young dragonflies eat baby mosquitoes.

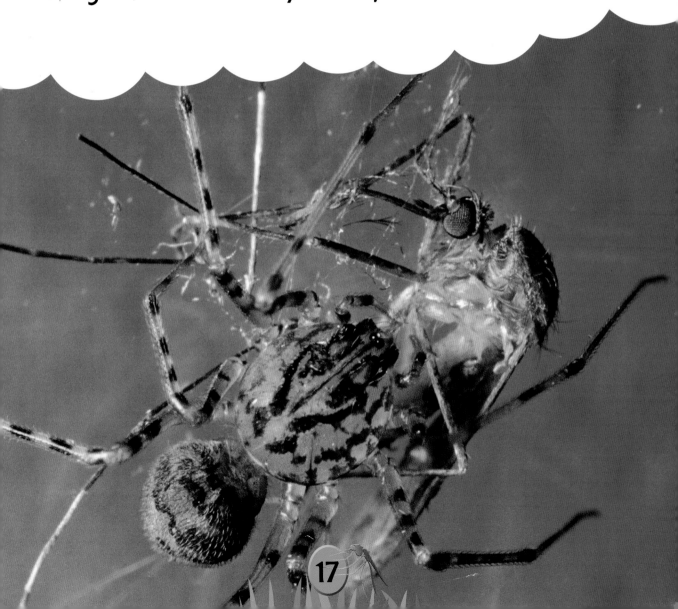

How Do Mosquitoes Move?

Adult mosquitoes can fly. A mosquito can fly a long way to look for food.

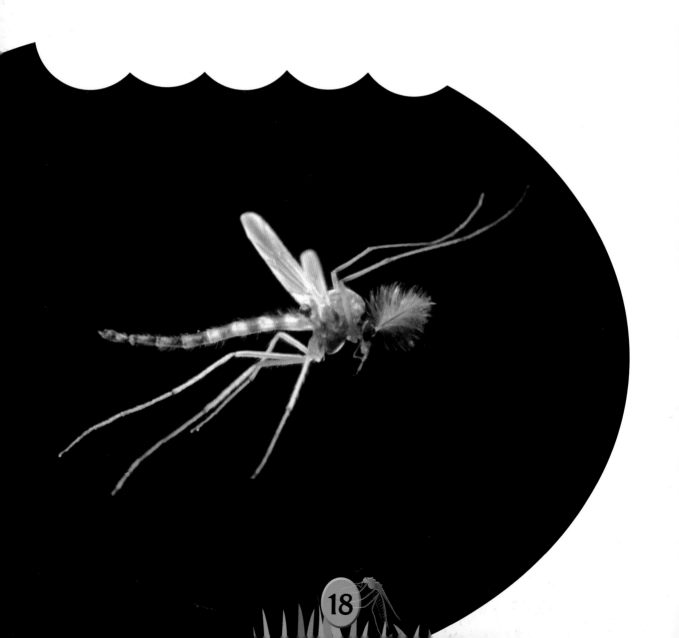

The moving wings make a whining noise.

Where Do Mosquitoes Live?

Mosquitoes live in damp, shady places, near pools of water where their babies can live. Even small puddles are big enough for mosquito babies to live in.

Mosquitoes often come into houses and rest on walls or ceilings. They live all over the world, especially in forests in hot places.

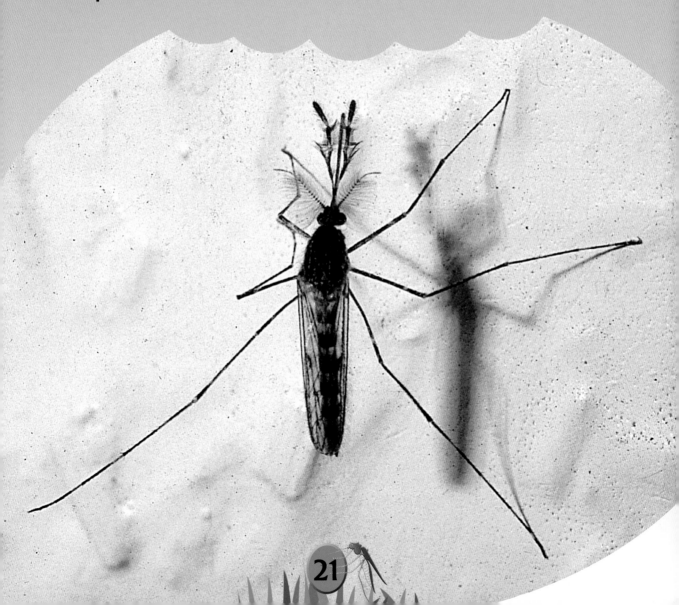

How Long Do Mosquitoes Live?

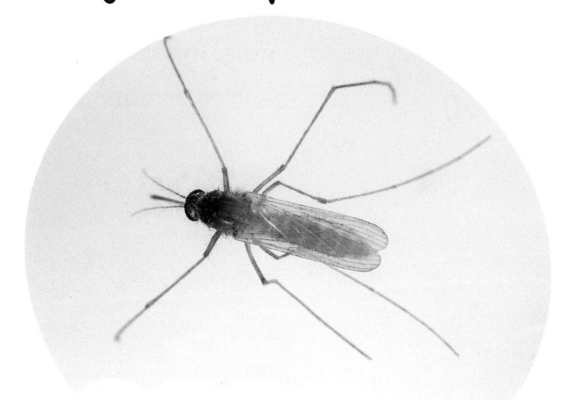

The **female** mosquitoes live the longest. Sometimes they live for two or three weeks. A few mosquitoes live much longer. They sleep through the winter in houses or **hollow** trees.

These mosquitoes lay their eggs in water in the spring and then die. In less than a month there will be new adult mosquitoes. Soon they will lay their own eggs.

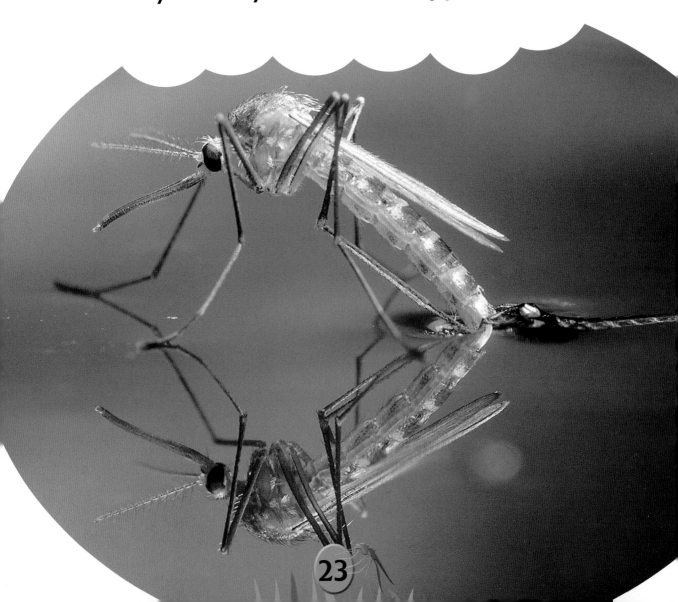

What Do Mosquitoes Do?

Most mosquitoes hide during the day. They come out in the evening when the air is cool and damp. They look for food and other mosquitoes.

Crowds of **male** mosquitoes dance together to attract **females**. The males listen for the sound of the females.

How Are Mosquitoes Special?

Mosquitoes are important food for birds and other animals. They can also cause harm. In some countries, mosquitoes spread disease, so people spray chemicals to kill them.

When a **female** mosquito sucks blood, she sometimes carries diseases from one person or animal to another. In some countries, people sleep under special nets to keep mosquitoes from biting them.

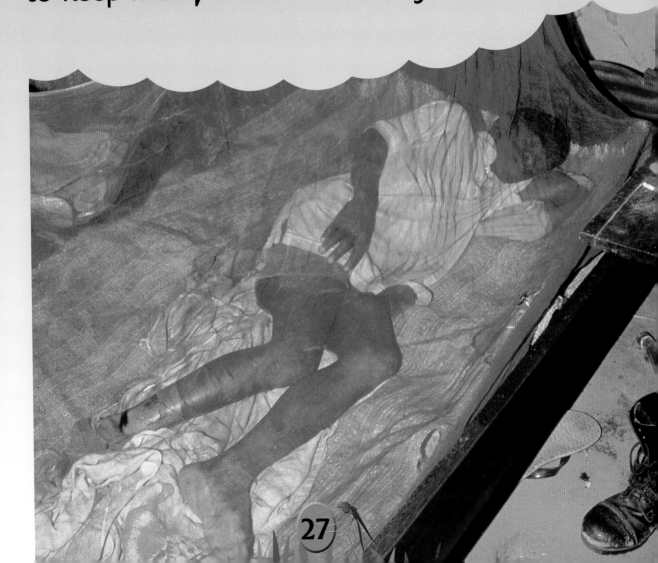

Thinking About Mosquitoes

Are there any large puddles or buckets of water near your home? Are there any tiny **rafts** of mosquito eggs floating in them?

Touch the water with a twig. Do any baby mosquito **larvae** wriggle away? If you can't find any, leave a large can of water outside in a shady place in spring or summer.

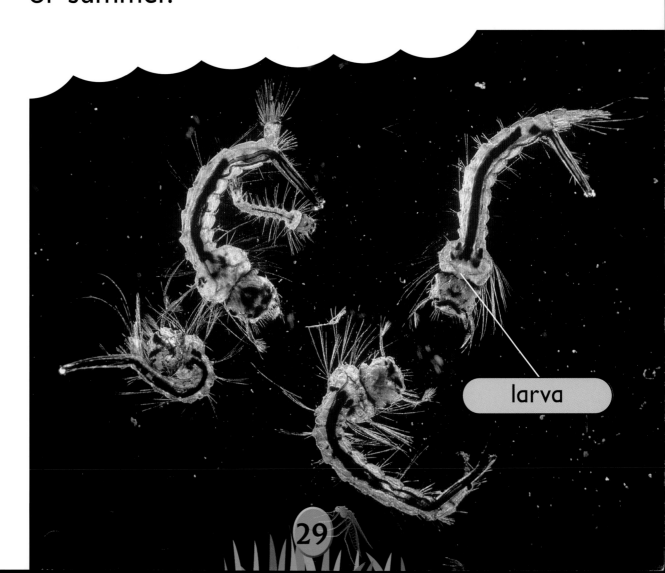

larva

Bug Map

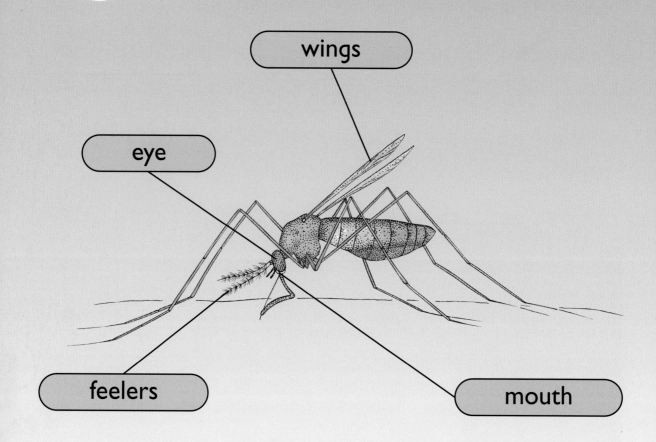

wings

eye

feelers

mouth

Actual size

Glossary

clotting when blood becomes thick, then hard, to form a plug that stops more bleeding

feelers two long bendy rods that stick out from the head of an insect. They may be used to feel, smell, or hear.

female girl

hatch to come out of an egg

hollow a hollow tree is usually dead and the trunk is empty inside

insect small creature with six legs

larva (more than one = larvae) little grub that hatches from the egg

male boy

nectar sweet juice inside flowers

pupa (more than one = pupae) older larva. The adult mosquito grows inside it.

raft something that is flat and can float on the surface of the water

Index

More Books to Read

Barraclough, Sue. *Mosquitoes.* Chicago: Raintree, 2005.